OVER COFFEE WITH THE MOUSE

Over Coffee
with the Mouse

Life and Leadership Wisdom from
32 Years at Disney and Beyond

Mark Rucker

HOUNDSTOOTH
PRESS

OVER COFFEE WITH THE MOUSE

Life and Leadership Wisdom from 32
Years at Disney and Beyond

ISBN 978-1-5445-2081-0 *Hardcover*

978-1-5445-2080-3 *Paperback*

978-1-5445-2079-7 *Ebook*

This book is dedicated to my father and mother, Richard and Carolyn Rucker, who, by sharing with me their solid values early in my life, laid a firm foundation for me. They taught me numerous life and leadership principles: the meaning of personal responsibility and what hard work looks like, that a happy life is not a life of excesses, that one should select friends carefully, to give my time and money cheerfully while saving and investing prudently, and what love looks like through their marriage.

They had the wisdom to provide us with more and more freedom as they saw my brother and me mature and make better decisions on our own. They also constantly made an effort to stay connected with us when we were out of their home, off to college, or out on our own.

They now love their daughters-in-law, grandchildren, and great-grandchild as much as they love their own sons. They have transitioned well from parents to best friends!

Contents

THE DAYS AS A DISNEY EXECUTIVE

THE POST-DISNEY DAYS AND REFLECTIONS

Disclaimer

This book is designed to provide valuable information and motivation to the readers. It is provided with the understanding that the author and publisher are not engaged to render any type of psychological, legal, or any other kind of professional advice. It is not meant as a substitute for direct expert assistance.

This book was not written in cooperation with the author's prior employers or associates, nor endorsed by them. The views, thoughts, and opinions expressed in the text belong solely to the author.

This book is not intended to use proprietary information or copyrighted material; any inadvertent use of such copyrighted material not specifically authorized by the copyright owner should be considered "Fair Use" as teaching and commentary under Section 107 of US Copyright Law .

No warranties or guarantees of completeness, accuracy, usefulness, or timeliness are expressed or implied by the publisher's choice to include any of the content in this volume. Neither the publisher nor the author assumes responsibility or liability for any errors, inaccuracies, omissions, or any other inconsistencies in the content of this book. Neither shall be liable for any damages, including, but not limited to, special, incidental, consequential, or other damages.

Introduction

Early in my career, my father told me about a "drop file" concept he always used. He said to determine what is important to you and create categories accordingly. Then, as you gain information, drop the materials you learn and encounter into the file with the corresponding category. I decided to use that system by creating a physical and electronic "Leadership" file folder in which I stored valuable leadership lessons I learned. This indirectly inspired me to begin to create a "Life Diary" in which I chronicled life lessons. This all ultimately morphed into a "Leadership and Life Lessons" file of wisdom I collected and shared along my professional journey, and that became the backdrop for this book.

Periodically throughout my life, I found myself

requesting a coffee chat with an informal mentor, respected colleague, my local pastor, our family's financial advisor, or a close friend in an effort to work through challenges or simply seek advice. As I advanced in my career, I found more and more individuals requesting the same of me. I loved those coffee chats where I could help a friend or colleague, often thinking those times were the most impactful and valuable of my career and my life.

Whether you are thinking about leadership, emerging as a leader, or advancing in your leadership responsibilities, I wrote this book to help you in your leadership journey by chronicling some of those coffee chats through real-life story sharing. The set of topics in this book are broad and sweeping, intended to offer you many quick servings of insight that can steer you toward a more fulfilling life and leadership excellence—even though we never had a coffee together.

This short book shares lessons and insights I learned along my journey, many positive and a few that are not. The motivation for sharing them with you is to help you become a better leader and person starting today and gain the wisdom necessary to avoid making many common mistakes and experiencing their attendant pain. I hope to encourage you, the reader, to become an authentic and transparent person who does not compartmentalize your work life from your non-work life. When you realize the benefits to be gained from this approach and commit to being this type of individual, it acts as a foundation for great leadership as an outstanding contributor at work, a better friend or family member at home, and a positive, contributing member of today's society.

So, in this digitally saturated age of broad, mobile connectivity with snippets of information coming at lightning speed, attention spans cut short, and a general unwillingness to read extensively, my hope is that you slow down, pour a cup of java, and truly enjoy this quick read, *Over Coffee with the Mouse*.

The Pre-Disney Days

A Love for Your God-Given Talents and Gifts

When my brother and I were young, our family was stationed at Vandenberg Air Force Base in Southern California, and we were the beneficiaries of great schooling and youth sports. It was there I started to realize I really enjoyed math, the German language, and almost all sports. But I also discovered what came easily to me: football was a grind even though I liked the sport, basketball was energizing, baseball was truly enjoyable, and tennis was euphoric. Over the years, I found myself spending more time doing what I was great at and loved.

In the years to follow, my parents would ask me

what I truly enjoyed and what I thought I excelled at. I also had a few teachers, a counselor, and a coach who went out of their way to encourage my talents and gifts. In fact, one of my earliest schoolteachers recognized my abilities in math and told me he thought I should become an engineer. He told me the areas a person excels in are usually the areas that person should endeavor to stay with, as they will bring them the most satisfaction and success.

One of my favorite movies, *Chariots of Fire*, magnifies this point in a poignant scene. Eric Henry Liddell, who was a British Olympic gold medalist runner, Scottish rugby player, and Christian missionary, says in the movie during the height of his running career, "I believe that God made me for a purpose [to be a Christian missionary]. But He also made me fast, and when I run, I feel His pleasure."

So **pay close attention to your natural talents and gifts.** Find wise people in your life who are willing to help you find where you excel. And by all means, as early as possible, experience different sports, take a wide variety of classes, work in many different jobs, and take advantage of various assessment tools (talent, career, spiritual) to understand yourself.

QUESTIONS:

What areas do you excel in, and are you spending your precious time enjoying those gifts and talents?

Do you have people in your life confirming your talents and gifts? If not, who might help you identify them?

In areas where you are unsure, are you assessing where all your gifts and talent lie?

Have Your Own Diversity Story

My dad was enlisted in the United States Air Force. As part of that armed services lifestyle, when you received a new assignment, you often moved to another base. So, early on, we as a family got used to moving and quickly meeting new friends and neighbors, as base families were fast to extend a friendly, Americana-style welcome. Later, I realized the people on the base had a common mission that unified them, and they extended the right hand of fellowship because they too knew what it was like to move to a new location far away from their last assignment. Happily, there was so much unity that my brother and I never experienced a racial divide. Our schools, sports teams, and extracurricular activities were blended together from a wide range of races and ethnicities. In fact, as a teen, the only diversity tension I experienced was the question, "Is your father enlisted or an officer?" (class or rank diversity).

This scene changed abruptly when my dad informed us he was retiring from the Air Force after twenty-one years and we were moving from California to Missouri to start our non-armed services life. The new environment was very different: (1) there was very little racial diversity, (2) there were cliques of every aspect (the intellects, the elitists, the jocks, the druggies, the nonconformists, etc.), and (3) many of the people in our new community did not trust people coming into their high school who, as they would say, "were not in our elementary and junior high school classes and teams."

There was one young lady who stood out, who was always kind and compassionate to everyone regardless of clique or newness to the city or the high school. I started to **learn the spirit of hospitality** from her style and actions. Through these tough but memorable times, I would later on commit to that same approach as I entered the hospitality industry, and as a leader, I always tried to create a welcoming, hospitable, and inclusive environment.

QUESTIONS:

There are many forms of diversity. What is your diversity story, and are you ready to share it?

What early life lessons have shaped you into who you are today?

Who stood out as a key influencer who positively shaped you?

Appreciation for Diverse Roles and Hard Work

In my preteen and teenage years, I mowed lawns, worked in all the positions at a movie theater, lifeguarded at municipal pools and school natatoriums, worked summer construction jobs, worked multiple positions in a lumber yard, worked at a pizza shop, and was even a doorman at a college bar. This wide range of experiences helped me understand the service industry, learn the technical aspects and processes of business, better understand life-safety concepts I would later use in my career path, and learn some construction trades that help me maintain my home today. Most importantly, they exposed me to hard work, taught me the meaning of **a fair day's wages for a fair day's work**, and gave me a **great appreciation for people who devote themselves to hard work**, sometimes six to seven days a week for months on end. (Little did I know that decades later, I would find myself in Orlando working six weeks straight, from mid-August through late September, during hurricanes Charley, Frances, and Jeanne.)

I believe it is this breadth of early work experiences and regularly moving between Air Force bases that prepared me to be flexible and adaptable throughout my post-college career. In fact, I was so conditioned for change that I found myself adopting the following mindset: "Put me in coach, any position." This enabled me to learn new aspects of various businesses, constantly work with new team members, and commit to improving the workplace safety, employee experience, customer experience, and business financials and processes at every place I worked.

This thirty-six-year professional journey has led me to success at three different companies, in about eighteen different roles in industrial engineering, information technology, finance, sports and recreation, transportation, and operations in the lodging and the theme parks industry; and as a regional and worldwide corporate leader. Now, amid the COVID-19 pandemic, I write this book and ponder what exciting challenges await.

QUESTIONS:

Have you worked in a breadth of roles that provides enough perspective and a basis for future career decisions?

What experiences and learning can you leverage in life or future positions at work?

How do you think about "fair wages for a fair day's work" for both yourself and others? What does hard work look like to you?

With life and the work environments changing so rapidly, why do you think flexibility and adaptability are important leadership traits?

Prepare Early for Life's Challenges

After making it through the first two years of core engineering "weed out" classes, I was in my junior year, finally starting to enjoy industrial engineering classes. However, I was struggling with two emerging realizations: (1) I was very different from my engineering classmates, and (2) I could not see myself being an industrial engineer for the rest of my life. I called my parents one evening that semester and shared my struggles, opening the conversation with, "I am not like my engineering classmates, and I am wondering if I should transfer to the business school." My parents' response was threefold:

1. **Everyone is uniquely made,** so you will not

be exactly like your classmates nor will any of them be like you.

2. Regardless of the school or degree you choose, **there will be both enjoyable and unenjoyable aspects of any subject**. And once you graduate and start working, the same will be true about either (or any) profession or job.

3. What you are learning now and in the future is preparing you to understand, work through, and sometimes even **solve life challenges**, not just prepare you for a professional career.

Now I look back at that conversation and realize all three were true for me at the time, especially the third one. In those formative years when that call occurred, the college experience was teaching me aspects of leadership I was too naive to comprehend until much later. I'm not referring to intellectual learning through select college courses or topics but instead other critical attributes a person can carry into future roles of leadership. For me, the college experience and educational training offered much more:

- Balancing **independence**, being away from home, and **interdependence** when working with fellow classmates on project case studies.

- Realizing the need to coexist and flourish in a culturally diverse and very **competitive** environment.
- Fostering a **drive for excellence**, even when feeling defeated (bad test scores).
- Dialing up **time management skills** and **prioritizing critical goals** for the day, the week, and sometimes beyond.
- Learning the **principle of moderation, balancing** class time with study time, social time, and work while remaining happy and healthy.
- Learning to convey thoughts or message simply and clearly when **publicly speaking**, rather than focusing on impressing others.
- Intensifying my own learning by **becoming more inquisitive and asking a lot of questions in class. Don't be shy** due to the fear of embarrassment. Often, your questions will provide answers to similar questions others had as well.

QUESTIONS:

Have you found yourself enrolled in schooling or engaged in work that you know you will not be involved with in the years to come?

Do you realize there are always enjoyable and unenjoyable aspects of every job?

Was there a time when you were learning and honing your leadership skills and were too naive to realize it? What have you learned that can be leveraged in other areas of your life?

The Early Disney Days

Balance Life's Priorities

When I was in my mid-twenties, I lived in sunny Florida, enjoyed my work as an industrial engineer at Walt Disney World, and had some great friends, but something was definitely missing. I learned from the prompting of a colleague at work and a caring Orlando friend that there was a God-sized hole in my heart. Through a series of non-coincidental events, I realized my life was empty and unfulfilling, and I was drawn into a personal relationship with the Living God. I learned of the interconnectedness and purpose of life and that I could not separate my personal life from my professional life nor my spiritual life from my physical and mental life. It was then I set my main priorities as my faith, my family, my work, and my community, endeavoring to do my very best with each while keeping the priorities in relative order of importance:

1. **My faith**—Make sure I put God first because He is the creator and ruler above all things. Make sure to seek the kingdom of God and His righteousness, and honor Him with my whole life. Love the Lord my God with all my heart, soul, mind, and strength. Love my neighbor (family, coworkers, community) as myself.

2. **My family**—Serve the Lord in our house, honor my father and mother, love and honor my wife, love my children, impart wisdom to my children and teach them to be loving and responsible, be selfless and submit to one another, encourage one another, provide for my wife and daughters while giving generously, manage our household well, dispense proper discipline for disobedience, strive for unity with our immediate and extended family, keep my word, and forgive one another. Bear one another's burdens.

3. **My work and community**—Choose friends carefully. Speak the truth. Be loyal and honorable, encouraging and hospitable, and kind and forgiving. Be humble, and count others

before myself. Sincerely follow good instructions. Seek the opinion of many good advisors. Be above reproach. Work diligently and heartily alongside my colleagues, promoting unity and teamwork. Use my talents to help others improve. Generate hope. Live peaceably, and bring parties together to solve problems. Envision the impossible. Be clear and clean in speech. Stand up for my friends and colleagues. Be generous to and demand justice for the poor and disadvantaged. Exhibit a spirit of love, joy, peace, patience, kindness, goodness, faithfulness, gentleness, and self-control—a lifelong process I continue to work on.

My new set of priorities helped me learn how to be a better son, husband, father, relative, employee, coworker, leader, community member, and neighbor. However, I also learned that many of these positive attributes could be leveraged in all areas of my life and were interchangeable between my roles at home, work, and within my community.

QUESTIONS:

Is there something missing in your life?

Do you compartmentalize your life?

Who or what do you put first in your life?

What priority do you place on family? Are you appropriately available for them?

Friends and colleagues heavily influence you and offer counsel. Do you choose them carefully?

Value—Discover—Empower

In the months following the discovery of my new-found faith, my belief in the value and worth of the people around me began to change drastically. I finally realized every human being is made in the image of God. Therefore, **every human being has infinite value.** I've also learned over the years that each individual was **uniquely made** and has their **own special gifts and abilities.** The secret is treating them as such and discovering what each person can contribute to magnify excellence.

If you are successful in discovering and nurturing the talents of everyone on your team, then as the senior-most leader, you can give away, or distribute, the power (empower) to your team members to do great things and accomplish the unimaginable. As the leader, you must always strive for equality but not position interchangeability (note: learning multiple roles is very positive, but a leader should never shirk their responsibility by having others do their job). You must also act with authority but not superiority.

When you think of team members and discovering their gifts, do not just envision your immediate circle of business colleagues. Cast a broad and wide perspective, including your extended business partners, in this net of interdependence. I found at Disney that every time my team would venture beyond our boundaries of daily responsibilities and seek the help of others, we would produce a better product or service, resulting in enhanced business performance and guest satisfaction.

This method is important to do and do right away because it fosters deeper relationships and levels of trust among team members. Also, in times of great difficulty, the people who responded most to this approach are the ones who will come to your aid. They will most easily offer forgiveness and tend to readily extend patience and grace when you need help in difficult work situations that require teamwork.

Value people by showing you care deeply for them by doing the following: believe in them, spend valuable time with them, encourage them, challenge them, trust and empower them, confide in them, and always be honest with them. Discover each other's gifts by spending time and building relationships tight and wide. Then empower your team to magnify excellence. We are stronger and more successful when we join together and depend on each other!

QUESTIONS:

Do you believe everyone is of infinite value?

Do you believe each individual is uniquely gifted?

Have you searched broadly and recruited a diversified talent set to ensure top performance?

Have you been fortunate enough to develop deep, collegial trust among your team that resulted in forgiveness when you personally made a mistake?

Stand Up for People

After being with Disney for about five years, I had the opportunity to serve in a downtown Orlando facility, the Christian Service Center, which was committed to aiding the homeless, rehabilitating prisoners, and helping them rebuild their lives and reintegrate back into society and our community.

I'll never forget an experience I had early on there. As I was leaving the facility late one night, a big, burly male resident asked me for a ride to the store. He needed to buy something for a job interview the following day. I agreed, and on the way there, I asked him how he found his way to this particular facility. He proceeded to tell me he had accidentally killed a man in a fight, was prosecuted and sent to prison, and was now working to get his life back on track. On the way back from the store, he asked, knowing I was a newlywed, why I came down to spend time with the men each week when I had a new bride at home. The only thing I could think to say was, "I guess God called me to show love and serve those in need, even manslaughter convicts." Thankfully, he burst out laughing!

That experience has stuck with me for three decades. It has always reminded me that the world, although beautiful, has so many heartaches and difficulties. There will be times when individuals are callously disregarded or discarded with no sense of fairness, equity, or respect. It also reminds me that great leaders have a responsibility to stand up for people, especially those in need: the helpless, the less fortunate, and even the less influential or powerful in the workplace.

I will close this chapter with one tangential thought on being available for your people. It is critical you make time to attend the most important events in your team members' lives when invited (e.g., weddings, funerals, awards ceremonies, etc.) and sometimes show up at an opportune moment to simply show your respect. They will never forget those appearances!

QUESTIONS:

Is there an opportunity for you to stand up for the most helpless, needy, and underprivileged in your community through loving service and justice-giving actions?

Is there an opportunity for you to encourage and ensure fairness, equity, and respect in your workplace?

Do you stand up for people outside your team when your team member is the challenge?

Do you prioritize making time to be available to your team, family, and friends?

I Do Know What
I Do Not Know

You hear a lot of businesspeople encourage their employees to continually improve or reinvent themselves. These improvements can relate to interpersonal skills, technical skills, or leadership. Early in my career, I learned the value of that advice when I was trying to justify a $70 million project. My boss asked me to pull together a financial pro forma to justify the capital expense, yet my undergraduate degree gave me only cursory knowledge of the in-depth financial information needed and clearly did not prepare me for this task. Because I had only one to two weeks to pull the assignment together, I knew **I could not accomplish this complex task on my own,** so I called a good friend who was a finance manager at Disney to **ask for**

help. Through her assistance, I was able to finish the assignment and justify the capital, but I took it one step further.

I followed up by sharing my recent story with another friend who was a well-respected finance director, **and I asked her how I might best shore up this weakness.** We talked about my capabilities and future ambitions and decided that an MBA was my **next, best course of action**. The next term, Disney sponsored my night classes, and I headed into the core curriculum with an emphasis on finance and human resource electives. The program proved invaluable throughout my career. I was so glad I had been in the business world prior to enrolling, as it enabled me to use real-world challenges to study while going through the eighteen-month program.

Just a few years later, I realized I needed to become more aware of my own shortcomings as a leader and that there were better ways to assess the talent around me. The Gallup Leadership Institute provided me excellent guidance in understanding my talents, gifts, skills, and abilities. It also taught me how to become a student of people. Needless to say, that was a weeklong turning point in my leadership journey. From there, I committed to becoming a much better leader. More to come.

QUESTIONS:

What shortcomings have you already identified and taken actions to improve or correct?

Are there areas where you need improvement and have failed to take actions to do so?

Think Big for Big Breakthroughs

I would often ask my team, **"What is your BHAG?"** A BHAG is a Big, Hairy, Audacious Goal.

I would encourage every leader in every industry to identify one additional BHAG they would like to accomplish by the end of the year—one that they would be surprised and delighted their drive and determination enabled them to accomplish. It should not be an individualized goal. It should be a goal that will require partnering broadly, leveraging many talents, and spending sizable time and financial resources to complete.

As an example, early in my career, when personalized bank cards were emerging, I challenged a Cast

Member on my Resort System team to find a way to leverage that technology at our hotel front desks during check-in. By the end of the year, this Cast Member proposed a solution where we could use this technology to encode data onto a guest's card that would enable them to gain access to their hotel room and our theme-park-entrance turnstiles and bill most point-of-sale charges back to their hotel guest folio. This was not only a BHAG for us but also a mid-1990s industry breakthrough. We called it the Key to the World card, and it was used for twenty years until it was reinvented and replaced.

In my time at Disney, I made an effort to assist each Cast Member in accomplishing their goals while taking on a BHAG of my own. Ironically, I was asked to assist in replacing the technology mentioned above with the Disney Magic Band as part of the broader MyMagic+ implementation in 2014. My role was on the leadership team implementing this suite of technologies and services in the final four to five months of development to ensure an on-time March delivery. Much was riding on this for our company, as public and media interest were very high.

QUESTIONS:

Are you willing to commit to one BHAG this year for yourself and each of your team members?

If you have already done this in years past, can you recall the feeling when the BHAG was accomplished?

My Leadership Break

By this time, I had been in four individual contributor roles and two leadership roles leading small teams of information technology and finance professionals. Because I was the finance manager within the sports and recreation division, I knew that a key water park leadership job was opening up at Disney's Typhoon Lagoon. And this was a type of leadership role I had dreamed about since I was in college. I kept asking myself, "Will they let a finance guy fill a key operations role?" Thankfully, I had prided myself and my team on not just being the best finance partner to the water parks team but also the "partners of choice" who went above and beyond by supporting nontraditional projects for finance Cast Members, such as business process improvement projects, guest satisfaction improvement initiatives, and many others. Our team was a confidant in most matters, and we studied the business thoroughly enough to have valuable contributing opinions. So I decided to apply for the job.

The panel interview was grueling: nine interviewers and two rounds of questioning. But in the end, I received a job offer! That night, I called my parents to tell them I just accepted my dream job. I told them I knew the business well, but I realized I had never led hundreds of people (peaking at around 450 in the summer) before, and that was my greatest concern. I recall my dad saying, "**Leadership is like adoption;** although you do not know them, you just welcomed 450 people into your family." He went on to suggest I learn their roles, understand their hopes and desires, share my values and expectations, and get out front and set a great example. He concluded with, "They will follow you when they see that." Looking back, the next few years were probably the most fulfilling in my life and provided some of the best development I've gained as a leader.

QUESTIONS:

Is there a role you were interested in but allowed doubt to keep you from pursuing?

Is there an opportunity for you to incorporate and practice an "adoption mindset" within your team?

Find the Right Person for Each Role

While in my first operations leadership role over a water park, I met and led many incredibly impressive individuals. However, there was one custodian who stood out above everyone else, and for the sake of anonymity, we'll call him Mr. B.

During the operating day, I would make a habit of visiting our Disney Cast Members and guests by scheduling time between meetings to walk and talk with them in the park. Mr. B was one Disney Cast Member who I especially enjoyed visiting, and I got in a habit when I saw him of saying, "Mr. B, everything looks so nice and clean! You do such a great job and do the work of four." He would always respond that he truly enjoyed the environment and the work, he felt he was put on this earth to clean, and it brought him great pleasure to do a good job and see others appreciate it. He would often go on to say that **it is important for every person to find what their personal mission is** and commit to doing it. He said that was much better than being someone who constantly grumbles about not doing what they enjoy each day.

That was a valuable lesson from a modestly educated man who had gained much wisdom and was kind enough to share it with me. From that point forward, I tried to **help people find roles they enjoyed, which ultimately benefited both the individual and the company.** This would come in many different forms: unhappy people who were misplaced by the company or who accepted ill-fitting roles; people who simply needed a change to bring a fresh perspective to their work; people who were growing impatient, as they were ready for the next challenge; and people who seemed to enjoy their role but weren't suited to perform well in it.

The last was always the most difficult to deal with,

as you had an individual who believed he/she was doing fine, but those around him/her viewed things very differently. In these types of situations, it can usually be distilled down to an issue of credibility. The team member either lacked the competency to do their job, were unable to communicate effectively to those around them what needed to be done, or had a personality trait or personal habits that were not well suited for the role.

What I learned very quickly, especially when you spend an average of two years in your leadership role before moving on to the next one, is that it is important to do the following:

- Assess the current business.
- Understand the organization.
- Make sure you have the right people in the right roles.
- Train your people properly.
- Empower the team to continuously improve.
- Measure the team's performance.
- Partner with others to achieve excellence.

I firmly believe ensuring you have the right people is of the utmost importance. All great leaders are committed to finding and retaining great team members. It's job number one.

QUESTIONS:

Are there people you work with who are absolutely the right fit for their roles? Are there those who are in roles they are not the right fit for?

Are you helping anyone find a role that is a better fit?

Have you, for the sake of expediency, placed wrong-fit talent in a role only to regret your decision later?

The 30-50-20 Rule

In my last role prior to becoming an executive, I had an outstanding senior leader who worked for me and prided herself on how effectively she developed her team members. In fact, she was so gifted in this area she believed she could equip and/or turnaround any Cast Member (we both eventually labeled it mouth-to-ego resuscitation).

She was determined to develop a certain Cast Member into a future leader. Our current HR director, who had incredibly keen individual perception skills, had also identified this same individual as extremely competent but was not as supportive of making them a leader because she sensed this individual had a tendency to subtly undermine others to the detriment of the whole team. My leader worked tirelessly over the agreed-upon two-month period to grow this individual into their new role, most often to the neglect of other pressing issues. Eventually, the true character of this Cast Member showed as not befitting a leadership role, my leader was exhausted, and she had other challenges arising due to the imbalance of time and focus.

The experiences I've had throughout my career and particularly as a leader led me to discover the 30-50-20 rule. Although this rule obviously is not hard and fast and the percentages differ by team, company, region, and even country, it states that about 30 percent of your team is going to be highly engaged and friendly toward change, new roles, and new key initiatives within the workplace. About 50 percent will hold a wait-and-see attitude and sit on the fence until positive momentum builds on the initiative. The balance of 20 percent will generally resist change and new initiatives and roles.

I believe it is critical, regardless of the percentages you experience and your level of optimism, to follow this formula:

1. Spend a majority of your time motivating,

directing, and developing the top thirtieth-percentile team members.

2. Ensure your leadership and the thirtieth-percentile team influence the fiftieth-percentile team members to rise to the challenge and aspire to excellence.

3. "Performance manage" the twentieth percentile, encouraging them to personally change and shift up into a contributing category or move on to another more-suitable role.

My senior leader in the story at the beginning of this chapter realized that not all people can be developed into leaders because some have underlying issues holding them back. This led her to identify whom she needed to focus on to optimize the performance of her entire team. Finally, she adopted a new philosophy with me: **Time is a leader's most valuable commodity. Be generous with it, especially with your team, but prioritize it wisely and use it carefully.**

QUESTIONS:

With whom are you spending most of your leadership time?

Are you effectively dealing with poor performers?

Know Yourself to Know Others

Just prior to receiving my first executive leadership position, I had the opportunity to participate in an off-site leadership assessment and development program. This weeklong course was divided into individual personal assessments and helping participants understand more about their team members: What was each member's gifts? What did our current team talent composite look like? How do you identify team strengths and weaknesses? What are possible suggestions to ensure a higher performing team?

The team assessment dived into core issues of:

- Ethics and responsibility

- Interpersonal style and approach with other team members and business partners
- Interactions with processes, systems, measurements, and organizational skills
- Levels of directional vision, concept, and strategy within the team
- Factors that enable team members to focus on delivering major goals and fuel them to do so

To say that week was valuable is an understatement; I would characterize it as an epiphany moment and turning point in my leadership excellence journey.

Not only did I learn things about myself that I didn't realize, but I also learned you need to **know yourself before you can begin to know others.** This empowered me to **do more of what I was great at.** It taught me to **surround myself with people who had different gifts and talents.** And it helped me begin to **be a student of people**, including team members, extended business partners, and even friends and individuals within my community. It was also the impetus for me to **assist those around me in understanding themselves better and beginning their own transformations within themselves and their teams.**

QUESTIONS:

Have you participated in a personal talent assessment?

Do you know yourself as well as you think you do?

What do others say about your leadership?

Does your own assessment of yourself align with the assessments of those you lead, your peers, and your leaders?

Has your team been assessed to ensure you have the optimal players and team blend?

The Days as a Disney Executive

Be Careful What You Ask For

During my time as General Manager of Sports & Recreation, which was probably my longest single assignment, my Vice-President would occasionally say to me, "Mark, when you are ready to transition to another role, just let me know." Part of this statement was related to company talent management and the other part was concerned with my development.

We had a solidly performing team, all business metrics were either very solid or moving into that range, and I was getting the itch to take on something bigger and more challenging. At the same time, I realized this was one of those special teams I didn't want to leave and would cherish for years to come. But when it's time to leave, leave and transition quickly into your new role. Do not look back, but remember the people who helped you get to that point.

So I eventually discussed with my Vice-President transitioning into a larger role within the theme parks or resorts division, leveraging my skills and experiences to succeed in a new position. Less than two weeks later, I was sitting in front of my current boss and my future boss discussing my next role. During that conversation, I realized I had been too general in my comments and hadn't specifically identified roles I wanted that I believed I would excel in.

As a result, I received an offer to move to a role that had a reputation of being one of the toughest at Walt Disney World: Director of Transportation. The transportation group operated the buses, boats, and monorails that transported almost one hundred million individual passengers annually. It was a union environment, where the transportation team serviced all the Disney hotels, theme parks, water parks, sports complex, and retail, dining, and entertainment districts. And when things were not running smoothly, it quickly became obvious to your clients and guests.

The role lived up to its demanding reputation, but fortunately, I recognized challenges early on regarding the organizational structure, talent alignment, and logistical systems. Therefore, we made changes rapidly and did not have to experience too many of those "difficult" days. This position really stretched me, and I am grateful for it.

Be careful what you ask for because it may be your toughest job ever. But then again, **it may be the best and most appropriate next assignment for your own personal and professional development**. Think it through carefully.

QUESTIONS:

Do you know what next role might best develop you and serve your career progression?

Are you owning and managing your career progression? Or do you think your company will manage it for you?

When you believe it's time to move to the next role, are you clearly conveying which role(s) you are interested in?

Wrong-Fit Talent Worth Retaining

Within a few weeks, I began to understand the challenges of my new organization and what needed to be done to "right the ship." The question was, "Is it appropriate to make changes so soon after taking the helm of a new team?" Normally, it was my belief I should take two to three months to ensure a good understanding of the people and the business processes before making sizable changes. But in this situation, the challenges were clear and the need was immediate.

The most obvious problem in my new department was there were **many leaders who were staffed in wrong-fit roles** (e.g., nonstrategic and nontechnical people placed in strategic and technical roles and vice versa). Due to this, I proposed an immediate organizational realignment with some slight restructuring. One person in particular was definitely in the wrong role. He lacked overall credibility due to technical incompetency and related communication shortfalls, but he was truly very sound in character.

Because of the organizational realignment and his subpar performance in his current role, some influencers were proposing his termination. But he had a wealth of experience, a broad and in-depth understanding of the overall business, and a great working relationship with all of the clients we served. The pressing question was, **"If we move him into what is believed to be a 'right-fit role,' will his performance quickly turnaround and will he truly enjoy his new role?"** I believe most people who are underperforming are, deep down, not enjoying the work they do. Thus, **great leadership has a responsibility to discuss, discover, and sometimes convince people there is a better role for them.** And when the leader and that individual mutually decide that is the case, everyone (the employee, his team, and the leader) is usually better off and happier in general.

Ultimately, he moved into a perfectly suited role that was less strategic and technical and leveraged his gifts and abilities. He came to flourish in his new role.

QUESTIONS:

When a team member is in a wrong-fit role, what is the leader's responsibility?

How does the self-awareness of the individual in a wrong-fit role play into the discussion and decision of reassignment or termination?

Are you the type of person who focuses on retaining good-to-great talent?

Difficult Times
Have a Purpose

Leading a team through great work and accomplishments is a noble cause. By this time in my career, I had already amassed many fond memories of so-called mountain-top work experiences: making changes as a young industrial engineer in manufacturing to improve the lives of the production worker, developing breakthrough systems and processes for our theme park and resort guests, launching one of the most-watched technology and services suite implementations ever, shaping a finance team to be the partner of choice, restructuring organizations to drive future excellence, and leading teams through expansion phases within the theme park and lodging businesses.

But I have learned in my life that when things are going smoothly, I often become self-absorbed and prideful. It is during these times that I need a strong reminder to take my eyes off myself, humble myself, and direct my energy toward the loving service of others.

However, it was the difficult times at work (and home) that probably shaped me most: navigating multiple serious family medical emergencies with my daughters and mother, eulogizing a beloved Disney colleague at his funeral, providing CPR to visiting guests and a fellow Cast Member, responding to fatal and near-fatal incidents involving my guests and Cast Members, and enduring multiple company restructurings in a short time frame that greatly impacted fellow colleagues' livelihoods.

My struggles are carved as deeply into my memory as the mountain-top experiences, and I have found purpose and meaning in both good and bad times. The difficulties I have experienced also taught me one can find and spread joy amid life's challenges. As an example, when I was in my most challenging leadership role, I one day rode on a Disney bus where our bus driver was singing beautifully to her guests. While disembarking, all the guests said to her, "You made my day and turned something ordinary into something truly extraordinary!" She taught me something that day.

In my next role, a few years later, some of my theme park Cast Members learned that a young, terminally ill guest had to leave our park early to rest at one of our hotels. Her deep disappointment that she would not see her favorite character turned into surprise and delight when my team orchestrated Cinderella's unannounced visit to her hotel room later that evening for a one-on-one meet and greet. Years later, while leading in a more challenging and complex corporate role (and one more removed from the daily Disney magic), I encouraged my team and myself to adopt the mindset of "serving those who serve our guests" as a constant reminder of earlier, valuable lessons.

I look back at those times and am sure that **difficult times are put before us to refine us, help us realize we all have a purpose in life, and present the opportunity to lead responsibly in the finest details and most critical situations.**

QUESTIONS:

When difficult times arise, where do you direct your attention?

What serious situations have driven you to help others (family, friends, neighbors, and even strangers)?

Do you recall and value valley-low experiences as easily as the mountain-high experiences?

Are you able to see glimmers of hope through extraordinary acts of service during darker times?

Have you been defined through difficult times? Have these experiences helped you find a more meaningful purpose? Did you lead responsibly through those challenges?

Development Feedback—Lead Where You Are

A few years later, I was moved to one of Disney's major theme parks and charged with leading the operations team, which included the arrival experience and parking, main entrance operations, attractions, entertainment, custodial, and international programs departments. One critical initiative was to assess the state of our frontline leadership, develop them to improve team leadership metrics, and identify those who were best suited for near-term, mid-level leadership development.

When this was announced to the leadership team, there was a frontline leader who came to my office expressing his excitement about the program and his future development. He also asked if I had time to talk with him about his career in the coming weeks, so we set up a career chat.

Interestingly, when we sat down, he immediately went into a superficial developmental-checklist conversation, listing everywhere he wanted to work and every assignment he thought would be good for his development. Further, he said he wanted to rotate through all the departments within operations, gain experience with one of the new development projects (which were plentiful at the time), gain exposure to labor planning, and be identified as a leader who participates in a park-wide committee. As I was listening, all I could think about was, his current performance rating was a low three on a five-point scale, and the consensus was, his team had low respect for him as their leader. So I said exactly that.

I said, **"It is important to dream, envision your career, and express ambition, but do not let your ambition outstrip your performance and capabilities."** I reminded him the most important job was the job he had today and **"great leadership**

with his current team was the most immediate springboard for future consideration and success." I also asked him if his current leader ever shared similar conversations with him, to which he replied no. Obviously, that prompted a second conversation with his current leader and a subsequent three-way conversation to ensure we were all communicating clearly and understood where everyone stood on this matter.

What followed was a series of follow-up meetings with HR and the department head to ensure his department was being properly led. Leading people is hard, but leading leaders and their teams is even more challenging. Be up for the call.

QUESTIONS:

Are you helping your team members understand what is most critical for their development and advancement?

Are your leaders communicating the same to their leaders?

Are you excelling in your current role and demonstrating capabilities for greater assignments?

Excellence Shows You Care

There was a more-tenured fellow executive during my time at Disney who would often recruit top talent from other teams within the company, then create a competitive environment to become the number-one team over the teams from which he recruited. This leader's approach inspired courage, activation, and a healthy level of assertiveness among his Cast Members. However, he also stirred up an unhealthy competitiveness and need to "outscore" other teams.

This approach was disheartening to leaders within his own team and disappointing to the members of the other Disney teams. To curb the disappointment of some of my team leaders, I would often say,

"We can strive for perfection, but as humans, we can never achieve it. So we will have to strive for excellence, and that will often be good enough. We don't have to crush the competition."

Competition is a good motivator, a fuel that propels individuals, but it often drives an outward focus. A drive for excellence looks inward and often results in a more satisfying journey to first place. Commanding excellence-instilled pride in my team, both corporately and individually, resulted in three outcomes: (1) it drove my team toward the higher goal of excellence, (2) it indirectly stimulated greater excellence among other teams, and (3) it ensured my leaders were being noticed outside my organization, often resulting in the attempted recruitment of my team members by competitive and not-so-competitive internal teams.

My favorite phrase I coined while working at Disney was, **"Hold on tightly enough to your team members that they know you care. But when they are ready to leave you for bigger and better opportunities within the company, don't hold on so tightly that it hurts your hands."**

QUESTIONS:

What drives you as an individual—competition, assertiveness, or maybe just the pursuit of excellence?

Is striving for excellence good enough for you?

How does striving for excellence benefit your team and the individuals on that team?

How do you show you care for your team members? Do you hold on selfishly or too tightly?

Act on Bad News

After taking a regional executive role, I was soon informed our business's safety scores were not what we had hoped or reported—and that was a huge issue since we emphasized safety as our first priority. My new manager, who was a direct report, went on to say, most leaders were overly generous in their scoring when self-auditing their areas, and their excellence scores were probably fifteen percentage points lower than reported.

Upon learning this, I privately and immediately shared this news with my leader and told her we were launching a five-phase turnaround plan: **Validate, Communicate, Activate, Eliminate, and Celebrate**.

First, it was important my new manager felt his

perspective and opinion were heard. So we moved quickly to sample audited areas to clearly **validate** or invalidate his suspicions. Unfortunately, his perspective was correct, and his estimates were spot-on.

Now equipped with the facts and details of the dilemma, the next step was to **communicate** with the affected areas, sharing the news, broadly raising awareness, and seeking support and concurrence with the regional plan.

The third step was to **activate** and institute a third-party auditing process to continually provide feedback and ensure the self-audits were more accurate moving forward.

This allowed the area leaders to see their own deficiencies and put action plans in place to self-correct and **eliminate** the problems they were now accurately observing in pre-opening, operating, and closing practices and procedures.

Last, when this new approach took hold across the whole organization, external and internal audit scores matched and area leaders owned and more proactively addressed concerns, making the environment a safer place to work and play. That is something to **celebrate**!

How do you react when you receive bad news?

Do you have, or is there, an appropriate approach to addressing bad news?

How does that approach ensure you minimize the possibility of it reoccurring?

Communicate, Then Honor Your Word

When I moved into my first global corporate role, I led a team of extremely gifted and capable hospitality line-of-business experts who earlier supported only US clients. Having never been structured with central, corporate, worldwide oversight before, there were pockets of resistance from certain regional vice-presidents and their teams. This should be expected because of the newness of the relationship, and most were highly experienced leaders within Disney and/or had been with other top-brand hotel companies in some of the most popular markets. Many didn't need the business improvement support.

However, as a new organization, we were tasked

with identifying or creating the best practices across our worldwide brand and assisting sites in achieving higher quality and brand consistency, where appropriate. Initially, this was most difficult for me and my team. But in our first global, face-to-face summit, I had the opportunity to explain, and even implore, that we were there to learn, understand their business challenges, and help them, not autocratically run their businesses from afar. Over the next few days, we shared our strategic plans, sought input from global clients, made adjustments to those plans, and formed agreements on partnered work and how we would effectively work together.

Through that experience, effective communication, and our commitment to serve them and honor the promises made, our relationships deepened. My leaders' and team members' jobs became a little easier, our clients more readily sought our support, and our team developed a reputation of being a humble yet extremely helpful group of hospitality professionals and partners.

QUESTIONS:

When your team is facing resistance or opposition, do you intervene to ensure their greatest level of effectiveness?

What approach do you take to deepen relationships and solidify partnerships?

How does clear communication and keeping your promises promote a good work environment?

Sustaining Hope— Flexibility and Adaptability

Late in my career, in December 2013, I received a call on a Friday evening asking me to lead a critical project with some extremely talented senior executives. This project had already been the subject of widespread rumors, was ultra-high visibility, was behind schedule, and had to launch in a seemingly impossible four months because the launch day in late-March 2014 was being announced in just weeks. As a result, our company CEO and segment chairman and president would be interviewed by many top media personalities.

I accepted the challenge, immediately left my

current role, and worked tirelessly for months with thousands of other team members who had already devoted much more than I had to ensuring the project's success. We painstakingly decoupled "scopes of work" that were not critical on launch day, believing they wouldn't be missed by our guests, and intensified our focus on "in-scope work," streamlining on-time delivery.

This prompted some uncomfortable conversations with peers and superiors who had vested interests in noncritical scopes, but they ultimately understood and supported this temporary decision in light of the circumstances and pressures. All this enabled us to deliver on time with fanfare from our guests and positive press from many media outlets.

Remember, **it is important to sustain hope in an organization by stepping up and stepping in to help team members** who have worked hard to accomplish shared goals. Even though you may have enormous funding, extraordinary talent, and the best-laid plans, **circumstances and life in general may require you to remain extremely flexible and adaptable to accomplish the goals** set for you and your teammates.

QUESTIONS:

Have you ever made a career decision that placed you in an extremely challenging situation that ultimately proved to be extremely rewarding?

Have you been in a situation that required you to coach your peers or superiors?

When have you had to exercise flexibility and adaptability to conquer a challenge set before you?

My Disney Connection

Over my thirty-six-year career, thirty-two years were spent with Disney in varied capacities. Because of its vast size and scope, I actually served and led in fifteen different roles during this time, with positions in industrial engineering, information technology systems, finance, water park operations, transportation, theme park operations, and global corporate resort lodging and parks. You may be asking, what causes an individual who enjoys change to stay with a company for so long? Well, I believe it is "my Disney connection." The same **type of connection each of you should be looking for** when you commit to a company.

As I mentioned earlier, during my father's career

in the Air Force, my family was stationed in Southern California. My family didn't have a lot of money, and the cost of living in California was, like today, VERY HIGH. Regardless, my parents surprised me and my brother by taking us to Disneyland in the summer of 1970, where we spent the night at the Disneyland Hotel. Although we watched the Wonderful World of Disney on TV Sunday nights, this was the first real-life, physical connection I had with Disney. Despite all the magical delights of Disneyland, for some reason, the Disneyland Hotel's Dancing Waters show, featuring emotionally stirring music combined with a fountain-and-light show, captivated me. Little did I know, or even dream or imagine, some fifteen years later I would be working for Disney. And crazier yet, four years into my career with Disney, a job assignment would take me to Disneyland, staying in the Marina Tower at the Disneyland Hotel, where I first watched that enchanting show nineteen years earlier. I fought back tears and then fully realized Disney really does create memories for a lifetime!

Well, now you know what got me hooked. But what kept me there for so long? Disney maintained four major values while I worked there, and I continually believed in them. They are:

1. **A Purpose Greater than Self**—Bringing families together to create memories for a lifetime.
2. **High Values Upheld and Lived Out**—Maintaining openness, respect, courage, honesty, integrity, diversity, and balance.
3. **World-Class Employees (Cast Members)**—Hiring and retaining the most committed and talented people across the globe.
4. **Commitment to Excellence**—Committing to excellence in all you do, from dreaming to creating, safety to security, planning to process execution, designing to building, financial planning to financial results, and caring for all (Cast Members, guests, community members, and shareholders).

When you make career choices, don't just focus on what you are great at; consider also what you have a passion for and what aligns with your personal goals. **Make sure the purpose and values of the organization you are joining align with yours.** And always probe these questions when hiring leaders from outside your organization.

QUESTIONS:

What deep, meaningful connections do you have to your current role?

What do you value most in your current work environment?

What is missing or lacking in your current work environment that you can positively contribute to improving?

Heartbreaking but Right Decision

I will never forget Friday, October 7, 2016, when my mother and father called to inform us my mother was diagnosed with Alzheimer's disease. Knowing the difficulty this would present to both my mom and dad, my brother and I began to talk to them about selling their home in Missouri and relocating to either the Denver metro area or the Orlando metro area, where my brother and I lived, respectively. Although they loved to visit my family in Florida, they despised the heat and humidity. So they made the decision to relocate to Denver.

This caused my wife and I to seriously consider moving to Colorado. We had already been dreaming of moving out to the mountain states, where my brother's family had moved many years earlier. But this would mean leaving Disney, as they had no corporate interests in Colorado and my role wouldn't allow me to commute. After thirty-two years, I quietly updated my résumé, and within two months, I had received an offer to be the COO of a midsize company in Denver. However, I didn't accept that offer because a highly regarded, ex-senior executive from Disney, whom I had worked with for twenty-eight years, asked me to join her company in Chicago. She was a great leader who was well respected in the industry, and her midsize company was growing rapidly, seeking top talent from *Fortune* 500 companies, creating a dynamic work environment, and building a respected family brand. So I joined her team.

This enabled me to move my home out to Golden, Colorado, to be near my family by way of Chicago for one year. My wife and I moved from our suburban home in Windermere, Florida, to a thirty-seventh-floor apartment in downtown Chicago. It was a dramatic lifestyle change, but we quickly discovered we enjoyed it, as we both had been growing complacent in Florida.

Many of my Disney colleagues thought we were crazy for leaving the most popular corporate brand in the world and the Florida lifestyle. Half thought Chicago was great, saying we would love the city from late spring through early fall but not the winters. But when everyone learned the number-one priority was to be available for family as the years advanced, they knew we were making the right decision.

Being open to making bold decisions and taking corresponding actions for the right reason(s) is always a good decision. We have found that doing so:

- Showed us there was a fulfilling life to be lived after Disney—a great life outside the magic bubble.
- Prompted us to simplify and streamline our lives by downsizing our worldly possessions before the move.
- Made us feel like we were "twenty years younger" by moving to the city.
- Enabled us to meet new business colleagues and great friends and positively impact their lives.

- Allowed us to move our home to Colorado and spend more time supporting my aging parents.
- Taught us that no decision will be perfect, as I greatly miss my Disney colleagues and we often yearn to spend time with our lifelong friends and dear family who still reside in Orlando.

QUESTIONS:

Does the fear of the uncertain or unfamiliar cause you to make no decision at all?

Have your circumstances forced you to be, or have you allowed yourself to be, lulled into a sense of complacency?

Have difficult decisions in life positively impacted you in unexpected ways?

The Post-Disney Days and Reflections

Help Others Pursue Their Dreams

When I left Disney, I believe there were more than 100,000 parks and resort segment Cast Members, not counting colleagues in Europe and Asia. Those who were able to develop great relationships and depend on each other to deliver excellence daily flourished. At my Disney retirement party, I pulled out notes from my diary to read to the audience, sharing specifics on how individuals positively impacted the lives of me and my family—name after name after name.

In the months that followed, many of my Disney colleagues stayed connected to me. I made sure I was available as a simple sounding board. I helped them think through difficult challenges, and I was there to provide sage career counseling. In fact, some would reach out to share they had either reached a stagnation point in their career or asked directly if my new company would consider hiring them. We ended up hiring over a dozen capable leaders in key positions or critical consultation roles this way, which contributed to our growth and helped each leader further their career and broaden their horizons.

Well, back to my retirement party. Most of my beloved colleagues were there, but some whom I hoped would be there could not attend due to conflicts. I read their names out anyway. This just punctuated for me that many people impact our lives, but often, you do not know whom you are affecting until events like this one take place. The lesson for me was threefold:

- **Be the best leader you can be for all to see, and as you are growing in your career, help others pursue their dreams as well.**
- **Remember your family, friends, and colleagues because they helped you achieve your goals and accomplish great things.**
- **Never stop loving your colleagues, friends, and neighbors (and even strangers).**

In the end, you will realize it is what you did for others that really matters!

QUESTIONS:

How have you helped others pursue their dreams?

Have you taken the opportunity to publicly recognize those who have helped you greatly at work and in life?

How do you show your love for your neighbors?

Be a Student of People—Emulate Great Leaders

Everyone enjoys working with and for a great leader. But sometimes we are placed with leaders who need a little help, need a lot of coaching, or simply need to get out of leadership positions.

If you are like me, you would rather observe the characteristics, traits, and styles of great leaders and emulate those than observe what not to do. However, I have found it is true you can learn a lot from poor leaders.

I count myself very, very fortunate to have had mostly good to great leaders in my life (at home, at church, at work, and in the community). With that said, I have also experienced some leaders who lacked the basic attributes to even be called a leader.

It is from great leaders that we learn what to emulate. So I want to start by discussing some of the most positive leadership experiences from my life and career in chronological order. Some of these people or professions might not normally be viewed as leaders or leadership positions. What is important is they exhibited leadership qualities that all should aspire to:

- Speech therapists and teachers who **committed to helping** me overcome a speech impediment during my preschool and early elementary school years.
- A middle school teacher who taught her students civics, government, and business **lessons in a fun way to prepare us for life**.
- A middle school physical education coach who would yell, "Hasten, hasten, time's a-wasting," **encouraging us** to pick up the pace during our one-mile runs and **make the most of life**.
- A high school German teacher who was able to make his students **feel comfortable** and made **learning** a new language **enjoyable**.

- A college engineering professor and counselor who was **readily available to assist** with educational challenges and **ensure his students' success.**
- A business owner, my boss in college, who taught me the workplace is highly competitive and **seeking wisdom and making sound decisions** is extremely important.
- Following college, my first leader, who was a very talented plant manager, **demonstrated humble inquisitiveness and empowerment, allowing me to bring new ideas** to the business he ran.
- My first Disney industrial engineering leader who **demanded high quality, high time and personal commitments, and a high level of service and delivery to clients.**
- A doctor and a great man in Orlando who **demonstrated a zeal for life, a sense of constant optimism, and an appreciation for a great sense of humor.**
- A finance executive who **helped me be more self-aware and counseled me on my personal development to equip me** for a brighter career future.
- An operations executive who **saw something**

in me early in my career and planned for my future personal, leadership, and team development.

- A senior executive who personally shared with me, **"When you make a mistake, learn from it, then put it behind you quickly and move forward with boldness."**

- Another senior executive who challenged me to see that **you have to get along with people during some of the most difficult situations to achieve success, whether they be subordinates, peers, or more-senior leaders**.

- An executive who demonstrated that **what a leader believes and what is inside a leader are infinitely more important than outward appearance**, and that is what team members appreciate most and loyally follow.

- A minister who showed **constant humility and taught me that you cannot please everyone or find comfort in the approval of mankind (Galatians 1:10)**.

- A senior executive who, although constantly understaffed and underfunded, showed me how to **create organizational capacity and an inseparable team environment through regular team meetings, clarity of purpose** and direction, sound communication, regular performance reviews, and an esprit de corps among his leaders and team members to spur on greatness.** He was also the type of leader who **trusted you implicitly,** and you got to know each other so well that each of you knew how the other would think or act—the truest of friends and closest of partners at work.

- A senior executive who **took an interest in me personally, both at work and in life.** She demonstrated **quintessential partnership and grace while influencing those around her.** She always **insisted on truth, honesty, and accuracy** in all we did. She was an individual who **celebrated my successes more than she celebrated her own** stratospheric climb and advancement and **wasn't afraid to share the truth with others in hopes of helping a colleague** without damaging their ego.

- A senior executive who showed unwavering integrity by **dealing promptly with illegal situations or immoral activities.**

- When in some of the most challenging and difficult situations, leaders (doctors, peers, business leaders, team members) who demonstrated true **empathy** and were **willing to drop every-**

thing and help me break through barriers to quickly resolve bureaucracies to assist my family or team members.

- A European counterpart who had a **deep trust in partnerships formed and worked with inseparable determination toward a common goal,** like a true brother.

- A US counterpart who **challenged anything and everything to demand the very best for his team, his customers, and the business.** He was also a **true entrepreneur** and the first to volunteer to try or test new ideas.

- A young college student we met in downtown Chicago who **demonstrated a great love for humankind** within that city, abroad, and in his distant country of Haiti.

- A brother who **listens intently** to help solve problems or offer counsel.

- A mom and dad who always try to **impart sound wisdom** amid life's unexpected turns and crazy situations.

QUESTIONS:

Do you learn leadership lessons more readily from great leaders or poor ones?

Have you learned leadership lessons from individuals who don't currently hold a position of leadership as you would define it?

Have you observed great leadership from individuals occupying positions of lesser, equal, and greater influence than you?

Be a Student of People—Identify Poor Leadership Attributes

It is from the poor leaders that we learn what not to do, and they often shape our "I never want to do that or be that way" mindset. I know they did for me. Fortunately, I spent the majority of my career with Disney, and the examples of poor leadership among the thousands of leaders there were few and far between. I have chronologically listed some of the poor leaders I have encountered, both at work and in my non-work life, to share with you the things they taught me about leadership:

- An **apathetic** high school teacher and coach who put forth little effort to engage or assist his students.
- Certain influential students (self-assumed leaders) in high school and college who **charted wrong paths and took wrong actions, taking with them either unknowing or willing followers** down to depths of despair.
- A leader who **never trusted anyone** on their team and **constantly micromanaged** even the highest of performers.
- A senior leader whose personal letterhead depicted a seagull dive-bombing the head of an individual. You can't make this stuff up! He was an arrogant and **combative** individual. He would visibly enjoy asking meeting participants to lock people out of the meeting for being slightly late. He would also periodically **confront and threaten people** for taking quick bathroom breaks, accusing them of wasting time.
- A leader who **used communication as a form of manipulation or control** and used deception and "guessing games" to achieve their desired results.
- A leader who talked the good talk but **lacked**

the credibility (character, competency, and communication skills) to deliver.

- A leader who **seized up when faced with making tough decisions**.
- Leaders who were **persistently negative**, possessing a "cannot do" attitude.
- Leaders who **wouldn't step up and say, "I made a mistake,"** hoping the truth would just fade away.
- Leaders who **wouldn't performance manage** team members, either out of fear of who the individual was or the simple unwillingness to take on the responsibility "for the good of the team."
- A couple of leaders who always **blamed the prior leader for the problems** in their area.
- Leaders who **used their team members** to deliver results but **didn't recognize the contributions of those members and took all the notoriety and accolades** for themselves.
- The leader who always appeared to be "all in" yet would **passive-aggressively** undermine good work behind the scenes.
- Leaders who were **unable to demonstrate care for team members or express gratitude**.
- Leaders who wanted to **fire people they did**

not like or who "were not their people," not because they were performing poorly.

- Leaders who would **regularly say yes but really meant no.**

My point here is, **great leadership is always more well received than poor leadership**. Also, regardless of your position or profession, **you are impacting people's lives every day** and just might be viewed in the eyes of others as a leader. So fight the temptation to emulate any of these negative traits or behaviors. Choose instead to leave a lasting, positive impression on those you lead or interact with.

Leadership is clearly not for the "faint of heart," but both negative and positive experiences can greatly shape you into an outstanding leader and person.

QUESTIONS:

What lesson(s) have you learned from a poor leader(s) that you never intend to replicate?

Have you ever seen a poor leader transform into a good or great leader?

Do you think direct coaching can impact a leader to change their ways?

The Importance of Nonglamorous Work—My Leadership Blueprint

I have had the honor and pleasure of being a part of new hotel and theme park openings all over the world, major attraction openings, major hotel renovations, and launches of new technology platforms. Those memories, and many of the photographs I took, are the ones I recall most frequently. I believe that's because I, like others, can get caught up in the misunderstanding that the biggest, most popular, and largest public relations events are the most important.

Not to take away from the importance of these huge events, but there are many other efforts that far exceed these when you take a close, hard look at them. I have broken them down into three areas of focus that I have used as a blueprint for my leadership approach:

1. DEVELOP AND PRESENT "YOUR BEST SELF"

- Envision the impossible without constraints, embracing curiosity and innovation, creating enduring excitement, and always remaining open to change.
- Unleash team members and harness their creative power to develop breakthrough ideas, designs, technology, and processes.
- Lead with a broad mindset, always thinking about the company brand and its position within the country and world, and collaborate with multifaceted and diverse talent.
- Demand excellence from people and products beyond what the team believes possible. Take on a continuous improvement mindset, challenging teams to do their very best.
- Lead so that people choose to follow you by trusting in them, being committed to their suc-

cess, celebrating with them, and always doing what is in the **"Your People"** section below.

- Demonstrate a sound character, showing unwavering integrity and ethical behavior.
- Demonstrate stability and optimism during trying times.
- Show a willingness to learn and grow through help from others.

2. TRULY AND FULLY LEAD "YOUR PEOPLE"

- Be clear about expectations.
- Make sure your people have the necessary resources.
- Empower the team to do great things.
- Recognize people for great work.
- Show you care through ownership, good follow-through, problem solving, and empathy.
- Encourage individual and team development, ensuring your people are learning and growing.
- Listen to your team members.
- Connect each team member's role to a broader mission.
- Commit to quality work.
- Create a friendly environment where people get to know each other.

- Talk to your people about their progress.

3. TOGETHER, CREATE AND OPTIMIZE "YOUR ENVIRONMENT"

- Create a safe environment for your employees and customers.
- Encourage your employees to be kind and hospitable to their clients and customers so that they want to return.
- Ensure your place is well maintained and clean for all to see and appreciate.
- Run your business in a financially responsible way, focusing on a smooth and efficient operation.

I believe it is not what you have done and experienced in life that is most memorable but how you have led and impacted those around you while accomplishing great things together.

QUESTIONS:

Do you place more importance on glamorous work over the nonglamorous?

What are some enduring aspects and positive outcomes of truly committing to nonglamorous work?

Do you have your own leadership blueprint?

Do you believe when you focus on and improve "Your Self," that positively impacts "Your People," who ultimately drive excellence in "Your Environment"?

Are you committed to lead people excellently while accomplishing great things?

Time Is Fleeting and Leadership Isn't Easy—Gain Wisdom Early

If great companies form diverse and talented boards to direct them, why not do the same for your life and career—they are just as important. If you haven't already, start building your "career board of directors" and schedule those coffee chats. Time is fleeting and leadership isn't easy, so gain wisdom in life and leadership as early as possible.

Now you know what I might say to you if we ever sat down and enjoyed a coffee together. Understand your natural talents, skills, abilities, and spiritual gifts. Be someone who positively impacts others' lives. Commit to working hard. Keep learning and preparing for life's future challenges. Keep priorities in their proper order. Value your people, know them well, and empower them. Stand up for people, especially those in need and the less powerful. Know your own shortcomings. Think big. Think of your team as family. Build a team with the right people in the right roles. Spend a majority of your time with those who are open to change or making a difference. Know yourself before studying others. Allow roles and assignments to stretch you and help you grow. Retain good-to-great talent. Allow difficulties to shape you into a better person. Provide honest feedback to others, and challenge them to be their best right now. Strive for excellence in everything to show people you really care. Don't shy away from bad news. Communicate clearly, and keep your word. Sustain hope by being flexible and adaptable. Select companies you join and organizations you associate with carefully. Always strive to make the right decision, even if the right answer is the toughest option. Help others pursue their dreams. Study, understand, and know your people. Formulate your own blueprint for life and leadership success.

Leadership is difficult. Parenting is difficult. Life is difficult. It is in difficult times that you will find your purpose in life and the opportunity to lead responsibly. Regardless of where your journey takes you and whatever leadership responsibilities you have, make sure you are the best leader you can be for all to see while keeping proper balance in your life and proper order of your priorities.

Time is fleeting. Leadership isn't easy. Do not live aimlessly. Gain wisdom in life and leadership as early as possible. My hope is, as you start or increase those coffee chats and put much of what I mentioned into practice, you too will be asked to reciprocate many times over. And there is nothing more important than being committed to loving care and service to others.

Acknowledgments

I want to start off by saying thank you to my wife, Stephanie, who has loved and supported me through our many life changes and challenges. Also, thanks for the help with this book. I also send my love to my daughters, Kristin and Lauren.

It would only be appropriate to recognize a few of the great leaders who truly shaped my career and positively impacted my life in this Acknowledgments section.

- *Kevin Myers* showed how to create organizational capacity and an inseparable team environment through regular team meetings, clarity of purpose and direction, sound communication, regular performance reviews, and creating an esprit de corps among his leaders and team members to spur on greatness. He was also the type of leader who trusted you implicitly, and you each knew how the other would think or act—a truest of friends and closest of partners at work.

- *Erin Wallace* took interest in me personally, both at work and away. She demonstrated quintessential partnership and grace while influencing those around her. She always insisted on truth, honesty, and accuracy in all you do and celebrated your successes more than she celebrated her own. She wasn't afraid to share the truth with others in hopes of helping a colleague without damaging their ego.

- *Select Disney HR executives and leaders* demonstrated true empathy and were willing to drop everything and help me and others break through barriers to assist my family or team members when some of the most challenging and difficult of life's situations arose.

- *Daniel Delcourt* had a deep trust in partnerships formed and worked with inseparable determination toward a common goal, like a true brother.

Thank you for helping me pursue my dreams and

impacting me greatly along my journey. I am so thankful our paths crossed!

About the Author

In 2021, I started my own company, The Golden Company, LLC, that provides consulting services predominately in the hospitality industry, including theme parks, resorts, retail, dining, and entertainment districts. It is also the business that oversees my authoring, publishing, and public speaking endeavors. As of 2020, I have been a board advisor for the University of Missouri in their School of Hospitality Management. Prior to that, I was SVP of operations and an executive leadership team member with Great Wolf Resorts, where I led the western US operations teams; established the corporate roles for rooms, engineering, and aquatics lines of business; implemented new enterprise-wide business processes and standards; and led the operations development team to support the US new-business growth strategy, including the opening of four lodges during my almost three-year tenure.

Prior to my time with Great Wolf Resorts, I had a fulfilling and successful thirty-two-year career working globally for Walt Disney Parks and Resorts and regionally at Walt Disney World Co. During that time, I rapidly moved through fifteen different roles with ever-increasing responsibilities. My various roles included global VP of experience planning and integration and VP of park operations, lodging, and operations systems integration. Some of my notable accomplishments included the product launch of Disney's MyMagic+, the planning and opening of new parks and resorts, the expansion of existing assets worldwide, and the driving of countless corporate initiatives. Other executive roles with Disney in earlier years included VP of park operations, Director of resort room operations, GM of park operation at EPCOT, Director of transportation and resort support, and GM of water parks and recreation.

I am a graduate of the University of Missouri, where I majored in industrial engineering, and I later earned an MBA while working at Disney. I currently live in beautiful Golden, Colorado, with my wife, Stephanie.

When I'm not consulting, you can find me babysitting our granddaughter, writing a few books, hiking, skiing, and enjoying all that the Colorado outdoors have to offer.